# POWER

# OF

# POSITIV

# E

# HABITS

*Transform Your Life by Adopting*
*Simple yet Effective Habits*

**Saint Abraham**

# Table of contents

## Maintaining positive habits
62

# Introduction

Max was a young man who had always struggled with staying motivated and organised. He would frequently find himself procrastinating and missing deadlines, which had a negative impact on his personal and professional life. However, one day, Max decided enough was enough. He made a commitment to himself to turn his life around by developing positive habits.

Max started small by waking up at the same time every day, making his bed, and exercising for 30 minutes. Over time, these small habits became ingrained in his daily routine and allowed him to build momentum. As he saw the positive impact these habits had on his life, Max continued to add more, such as reading for 30 minutes each day and preparing healthy meals in advance.

Max's newfound discipline and focus allowed him to excel in his career. He was now more productive, and his boss took notice, leading to several promotions and a significant increase in pay. Max's newfound success also improved his relationships with friends and family, as he was able to be more present and attentive.

Max was amazed at how the power of positive habits had transformed his life. He was now happier, healthier, and more successful than he ever thought possible. He often reflected on how just a few small changes in his daily routine had led to such a significant impact on his life and was grateful for the decision he made to turn things around.

Max was a young man who had always struggled with staying motivated and organised. He would frequently find himself procrastinating and missing deadlines, which had a negative impact on his personal and professional life. However, one day, Max decided enough was enough. He made a commitment to himself to turn his life around by developing positive habits.

Max started small by waking up at the same time every day, making his bed, and exercising for 30 minutes. Over time, these small habits became ingrained in his daily routine and allowed him to build momentum. As he saw the positive impact these habits had on his life, Max continued to add more, such as reading for 30 minutes each day and preparing healthy meals in advance.

Max's newfound discipline and focus allowed him to excel in his career. He was now more productive, and his boss took notice, leading to several promotions and a significant increase in pay. Max's newfound success also improved his relationships with friends and family, as he was able to be more present and attentive.

Max was amazed at how the power of positive habits had transformed his life. He was now happier, healthier, and more successful than he ever thought possible. He often reflected on how just a few small changes in his daily routine had led to such a significant impact on his life and was grateful for the decision he made to turn things around.

Positive habits have the power to shape our lives in profound ways. From improving our health and well-being, to boosting our productivity and success, the right habits can help us achieve our goals and live our best lives.

Whether it's taking a few minutes each day to meditate, or consistently eating a healthy breakfast, small changes can have a big impact over time. By embracing positive habits and making them a part of our daily routines, we can cultivate the habits that will empower us to reach new heights and live a more fulfilling life.

It also has the power to transform our lives in countless ways. They help us cultivate better relationships, reach our goals, increase our productivity and overall happiness. Whether it's developing a daily exercise routine, practising gratitude or prioritising self-care, small changes in our daily habits can have a profound impact on the direction of our lives. In this guide, we'll explore the benefits of positive habits and how to form them, so you can start living your best life, one habit at a time.

Chapter 1

# The Power of Positive Habits

Habits are powerful tools that shape our lives in numerous ways. They are the building blocks of our daily routines and can be used to create positive outcomes in every aspect of our lives, including our mental and physical health, relationships, and career success. The power of positive habits lies in their ability to create positive feedback loops, where small and consistent actions can lead to big results over time.

Positive habits start with small, achievable goals. These goals are easy to reach, and the satisfaction and motivation that comes from reaching them helps create momentum. For example, starting each day with a simple workout routine or a few minutes of meditation can lead to feeling more energized and focused. As you continue to build on these small habits, they become ingrained and eventually become part of your routine.

One of the most important aspects of creating positive habits is to focus on doing them consistently. Consistency is key because it ensures that the positive impact of your habits grows over time. By doing a positive action every day, you start to form a pattern that becomes part of your subconscious mind. This makes it easier to maintain the habit, even in the face of distractions or temptations. For example, if you make it a habit to eat a healthy breakfast each morning, you will soon find that you have less of a craving for unhealthy food and that you have more energy to start your day.

Positive habits also help us to become more intentional about our lives. When we engage in positive habits, we are making an intentional decision to do something good for ourselves and others. This helps us to focus on what is important in our lives and to let go of distractions and negative thoughts. By focusing on positive habits, we can start to shift our mindset to a more optimistic and hopeful one, which can have a profound impact on our overall happiness and well-being.

Another benefit of positive habits is that they help us to build resilience and increase our ability to cope with stress and challenges. When we engage in positive habits, we are strengthening our ability to handle life's challenges and setbacks. For example, if we make it a habit to exercise regularly, we are not only improving our physical health, but we are also increasing our ability to handle stress and cope with challenging situations. This increased resilience helps us to remain optimistic and motivated, even in the face of adversity.

In addition to the benefits we see in our individual lives, positive habits can also have a positive impact on our relationships and the people around us. When we engage in positive habits, we are more likely to be kind and patient, to communicate effectively, and to build strong relationships with others. This can have a ripple effect, leading to a more positive and supportive community.

positive habits are powerful tools that can shape our lives in profound ways. By starting with small and achievable goals and focusing on consistency, we can create positive feedback loops that lead to big results over time. Whether we are looking to improve our physical and mental health, build strong relationships, or achieve success in our careers, the power of positive habits cannot be underestimated. By making positive habits a priority, we can create a better and more fulfilling life for ourselves and those around us.

# Importance of positive habits

Positive habits are crucial for leading a fulfilling and productive life. They provide structure and routine to our daily lives and can greatly impact our mental and physical wellbeing. By forming positive habits, we can increase our levels of happiness, reduce stress and anxiety, and improve our overall quality of life. In this article, we'll explore the importance of positive habits and why it's essential to incorporate them into our daily routines.

- **Improved Mental Health**

One of the most significant benefits of positive habits is the improvement they bring to our mental health. Habits such as regular exercise, meditation, and journaling have been shown to have a positive impact on our mood and well-being. These activities promote the release of feel-good chemicals in the brain, such as endorphins, which can help to alleviate stress, anxiety, and depression. Regular exercise also improves sleep quality, which can further improve our mood and overall mental health.

- **Increased Productivity**

Positive habits can also increase our productivity and efficiency. By creating a structured routine, we can eliminate distractions and increase our focus and concentration. Good habits such as regular exercise and a healthy diet can improve our physical and mental energy levels, allowing us to be more productive throughout the day. Additionally, habits like setting goals and prioritising tasks can help us to better manage our time and achieve our goals.

- **Better Physical Health:** Positive habits play a crucial role in maintaining and improving our physical health. Habits such as regular exercise, healthy eating, and getting enough sleep are essential for promoting physical well-being. Regular exercise can help to improve cardiovascular health, strengthen bones and muscles, and reduce the risk of chronic diseases. A healthy diet, on the other hand, provides our bodies with the essential nutrients and vitamins it needs to function optimally. Getting enough sleep is also crucial for physical and mental rejuvenation, as it allows our bodies to recover from the daily strain and stress.

- **Improved Relationships**

Positive habits can also improve our relationships and social interactions. Habits such as being more mindful, practising empathy, and being more present in our interactions with others can help to strengthen our relationships and build more meaningful connections. Additionally, habits like setting aside dedicated time for family and friends and being more organised and reliable can help us to be more present and available for the people in our lives.

- **Increased Confidence and Self-Esteem**

Finally, positive habits can help to increase our confidence and self-esteem. By incorporating healthy habits into our daily routine, we can develop a sense of control over our lives and feel more in control of our surroundings. As we achieve our goals and see the positive impact of our habits, our confidence and self-esteem will grow, allowing us to tackle new challenges with a more positive and confident outlook.

In conclusion, positive habits play a crucial role in our overall well-being and happiness. Whether it's improving our mental and physical health, increasing our productivity and efficiency, or strengthening our relationships and self-esteem, positive habits can have a profound impact on our lives. By incorporating them into our daily routines, we can create a more fulfilling and productive life for ourselves and those around us.

*Power of positive habits*

Chapter 2

# Understanding Positive Habits

Positive habits are behaviours that are repetitive, intentional, and provide benefits for individuals in the long run. These habits are usually established through consistent and deliberate actions, gradually becoming a natural part of one's daily routine. Positive habits can be developed in different areas of life, including physical, emotional, mental, and spiritual. By understanding positive habits and how they can be formed, individuals can achieve their personal and professional goals, improve their well-being, and create a more fulfilling life.

One of the key components of positive habits is consistency. The more consistent a behaviour is, the more likely it is to become a habit. This means that individuals need to engage in the behaviour regularly and make it a priority in their daily routines. The repetition helps to solidify the habit, making it easier for individuals to maintain it over time.

Another important aspect of positive habits is that they are intentional. People need to have a clear purpose for why they want to develop a particular habit and be mindful of how it will benefit their lives. This awareness helps to keep individuals motivated and committed to forming the habit, even when it is challenging.

Physical habits, such as exercising regularly or eating a healthy diet, can have a significant impact on one's health and well-being. Exercise has been shown to improve physical fitness, boost mood, and reduce stress, while a healthy diet can help prevent chronic diseases and promote overall health.

Emotional habits, such as practising gratitude, self-care, and mindfulness, can also have a positive impact on one's well-being. Gratitude can help individuals appreciate the good things in their lives, boost their mood, and foster relationships with others. Self-care activities, such as getting enough sleep, eating well, and engaging in leisure activities, can reduce stress, improve mood, and help individuals feel refreshed and recharged. Mindfulness, on the other hand, involves being present in the moment and paying attention to one's thoughts and feelings. This can help individuals manage stress, improve their relationships, and increase their overall happiness and well-being.

Mental habits, such as setting and working towards goals, continuous learning, and reading regularly, can help individuals improve their cognitive abilities and enhance their knowledge and skills. Setting and working towards goals can help individuals focus their efforts and create a sense of purpose and direction in life. Continuous learning and reading can keep the mind active and prevent cognitive decline, as well as provide individuals with new information and perspectives.

Spiritual habits, such as meditation, prayer, and volunteering, can help individuals connect with a higher power, develop a sense of purpose, and improve their overall well-being. Meditation and prayer can help individuals quiet their minds, reduce stress, and connect with their inner selves. Volunteering, on the other hand, can help individuals give back to their communities, foster relationships, and create a sense of meaning and purpose.

In conclusion, positive habits are behaviours that are repetitive, intentional, and provide benefits for individuals in the long run. They can be developed in different areas of life and have the potential to improve one's physical, emotional, mental, and spiritual well-being. By understanding positive habits and making a conscious effort to form them, individuals can achieve their goals, increase their happiness and well-being, and create a more fulfilling life.

## How Positive Habits Work

Habits are repetitive actions that are performed automatically in response to specific triggers. They are a fundamental part of human behaviour and play a significant role in shaping our daily lives. Habits can be both good and bad, and they can have a profound impact on our health, relationships, and success.

The science behind habits is rooted in the idea of classical conditioning, a psychological principle first described by Ivan Pavlov. Classical conditioning refers to the process by which an unconditioned response (such as salivating in response to food) becomes associated with a new stimulus (such as a bell ringing). This process can be used to explain how habits are formed.

Habits typically start with a trigger, also known as a cue. The trigger signals the brain to initiate a particular behaviour. For example, the smell of freshly brewed coffee may trigger a person to start their morning routine. Over time, the behaviour becomes automatic, and the person no longer has to consciously think about performing it.

Once a habit is formed, it is maintained through a process called reinforcement. Reinforcement is shaping our daily lives. They are formed through classical conditioning and reinforced by rewards.

Habits can be difficult to change, but they can be modified by identifying the cue and reward associated with the behaviour and modifying the routine. Understanding how habits work can help individuals make positive changes in their lives and achieve their goals.

# Chapter 3

## Developing Positive Habits

Positive habits are actions and behaviours that have a positive impact on our daily lives, leading to increased well-being, success, and happiness. These habits are crucial in helping us achieve our goals, live healthier, and be more productive. Here are some positive habits that you can develop to improve your life:

**Exercise**: Regular exercise has numerous benefits, including improved physical and mental health, reduced stress, and increased energy levels. Whether you prefer going to the gym, running, swimming, or taking up a sport, making exercise a part of your routine can have a significant impact on your overall health and well-being.

**Good nutrition:** Eating a well-balanced diet that is rich in nutrients, vitamins, and minerals is essential for maintaining good health. Incorporating fresh fruits and vegetables, lean protein, and whole grains into your diet can help you maintain a healthy weight, reduce your risk of chronic diseases, and improve your overall energy levels.

**Hydration**: Drinking plenty of water is crucial for our health and well-being. Staying hydrated helps regulate body temperature, flush out toxins, and maintain proper bodily functions. Aim to drink at least eight glasses of water a day to ensure you are adequately hydrated.

**Good sleep:** Getting enough sleep is essential for physical and mental health. A lack of sleep can lead to fatigue, decreased concentration and productivity, and an increased risk of chronic illnesses such as obesity and depression. Aim to get 7-9 hours of sleep each night to ensure you feel refreshed and ready to tackle the day ahead.

**Gratitude:** Practising gratitude means acknowledging and appreciating the good things in your life. Whether it is expressing gratitude for your friends and family, for your health, or for simple pleasures such as a sunny day, this habit has been shown to improve mood, reduce stress, and increase overall happiness.

**Mindfulness**: Mindfulness is the practice of paying attention to the present moment, without judgement. It has been shown to reduce stress, improve mood, and increase overall well-being. Incorporating mindfulness into your daily routine can be as simple as taking a few minutes each day to focus on your breathing, or taking a mindful walk in nature.

**Reading:** Reading is a wonderful way to improve knowledge and expand your horizons. Whether you prefer fiction or nonfiction, reading can help you relax, escape from daily stress, and gain new perspectives. Incorporating reading into your daily routine can also improve vocabulary, concentration, and cognitive abilities.

**Time management:** Effective time management involves prioritising tasks, setting achievable goals, and using time wisely. This habit can help reduce stress, increase productivity, and improve overall quality of life. Make a to-do list each day and prioritise tasks based on importance and urgency, to ensure you stay on track and make the most of your time.

**Kindness:** Practising kindness and compassion towards others has been shown to improve mood and increase overall well-being. Whether it is helping a neighbour, volunteering, or simply smiling at someone, incorporating acts of kindness into your daily routine can have a significant impact on the lives of others and your own happiness.

In conclusion, developing positive habits can have a profound impact on our daily lives. From improving physical and mental health to reducing stress and increasing happiness, positive habits are key to leading a fulfilling and productive life. Incorporating these habits into your daily routine may take some effort, but the rewards are well worth it.

## Identifying Positive Habits

Positive habits are the actions or behaviours that bring us closer to our goals, improve our physical and mental health, and enhance our overall well-being. They can be small, such as drinking a glass of water every morning or stretching before bed, or more significant, like going to the gym regularly or learning a new skill. Identifying positive habits is a crucial step towards personal growth and development.

Here are some tips to help you identify positive habits:

**Identify your values**: Understanding your core values and what is most important to you can help you determine which habits align with your values. For example, if you value health and wellness, you may prioritise eating healthy and exercising regularly.

**Reflect on your daily routines**: Take a step back and observe your daily routines and habits. Look for patterns in your behaviour and consider whether these habits are serving you or holding you back.

**Set goals:** Once you have a good understanding of your values and daily routines, set goals for yourself that align with your values. For example, if your goal is to be more productive, you may consider incorporating habits like prioritising tasks, taking breaks, and avoiding distractions.

**Track your progress**: Keeping a log of your habits can help you stay accountable and track your progress. You can use a habit tracker app, journal, or even a sticky note to keep track of the habits you want to form.

**Surround yourself with positive influences:** Surrounding yourself with people who have positive habits and support your goals can help you build new habits. Seek out role models who embody the habits you want to adopt, and consider joining a group or community that shares your values.

**Be patient**: Habits take time to form, so be patient and persistent in your pursuit of positive habits. It's also important to remember that it's okay to slip up from time to time and that the process of forming habits is not always linear.

**Reward yourself:** Finally, remember to reward yourself for your progress. This can help reinforce the positive habits you're forming and make the process of forming habits more enjoyable.

forming positive habits is a crucial aspect of personal growth and development. By identifying your values, reflecting on your daily routines, setting goals, tracking your progress, surrounding yourself with positive influences, being patient, and rewarding yourself, you can develop habits that will help you achieve your goals and improve your overall well-being.

# Setting Realistic Goals

Setting goals is a critical step towards personal and professional growth, but it's important to set goals that are realistic and achievable. Realistic goals are specific, measurable, and have a clear timeline, which helps you stay motivated and focused on your progress. Here are some tips to help you set realistic goals:

Identify your values: Before setting goals, it's essential to understand your values and what's most important to you. This will help you determine the goals that align with your values and give you a sense of purpose.

Assess your current situation: Take a step back and assess your current situation, including your skills, strengths, weaknesses, and limitations. This will help you identify the goals that are feasible and within reach.

Set SMART goals: SMART goals are Specific, Measurable, Achievable, Relevant, and Time-bound. When setting goals, make sure they meet these criteria, as this will help you stay focused and motivated.

Prioritise your goals: Once you have a list of goals, prioritise them based on their importance and feasibility. This will help you focus your efforts and ensure that you're making progress on the goals that matter most to you.

Break down large goals into smaller, achievable steps: Large goals can feel overwhelming, so it's important to break them down into smaller, more manageable steps. This will help you stay focused and make progress towards your larger goals.

Create a plan of action: Once you have set your goals, create a plan of action that outlines the steps you'll take to achieve them. This will help you stay organised and focused on your progress.

Stay flexible: It's important to remember that life can be unpredictable, and goals may change over time. Be open to adjusting your goals if circumstances change, and don't be afraid to seek help if you need it.

Celebrate your progress: Finally, it's important to celebrate your progress and reward yourself for your achievements. This will help you stay motivated and maintain a positive outlook.

In conclusion, setting realistic goals is an essential step towards personal and professional growth. By identifying your values, assessing your current situation, setting SMART goals, prioritising your goals, breaking down large goals into smaller steps, creating a plan of action, staying flexible and celebrating your progress, you can set goals that are achievable and help you make meaningful progress toward your goal

## Building Positive Habits into your Routine

Building positive habits into your daily routine is a powerful way to improve your physical and mental health, increase your productivity, and enhance your overall well-being. Positive habits are behaviours that become automatic over time and require little conscious effort. Here are some tips to help you build positive habits into your routine:

Start small: It's easier to form new habits when you start with small, manageable steps. For example, if you want to exercise more, start with just 10 minutes a day and gradually increase the duration as you get used to the habit.

Make it a part of your daily routine: Incorporating a new habit into your daily routine makes it easier to remember and helps you build momentum. For example, you could make a habit of drinking a glass of water as soon as you wake up or stretching before bed.

Use reminders: Reminders can be a helpful tool to keep you on track and ensure that you don't forget to engage in your new habit. For example, you could set an alarm on your phone or leave a sticky note on your bathroom mirror as a reminder to drink water.

Surround yourself with positive influences: Surrounding yourself with people who have positive habits and support your goals can help you build new habits. Seek out role models who embody the habits you want to adopt and consider joining a group or community that shares your values.

Be persistent: Habits take time to form, and it's important to be persistent and patient in your pursuit of positive habits. It's also important to remember that it's okay to slip up from time to time and that the process of forming habits is not always linear.

Track your progress: Keeping a log of your habits can help you stay accountable and track your progress. You can use a habit tracker app, journal, or even a sticky note to keep track of the habits you want to form.

Reward yourself: Finally, remember to reward yourself for your progress. This can help reinforce the positive habits you're forming and make the process of forming habits more enjoyable.

In conclusion, building positive habits into your daily routine is a powerful way to improve your physical and mental health, increase your productivity, and enhance your overall well-being. By starting small, making it a part of your daily routine, using reminders, surrounding yourself with positive influences, being persistent, tracking your progress, and rewarding yourself, you can develop habits that will help you achieve your goals and improve your overall well-being.

## Staying Motivated

Staying motivated can be a challenge, especially in the face of obstacles and setbacks. But with the right strategies, you can maintain your drive and stay focused on your goals. Here are a few tips for staying motivated:

Set clear, achievable goals: When you have a specific, well-defined objective in mind, it's easier to stay motivated. Make sure your goals are realistic and attainable, and break them down into smaller, manageable tasks. This way, you can see progress and feel a sense of accomplishment along the way.

Celebrate your successes: No matter how small, it's important to acknowledge and celebrate your achievements. This will give you a sense of pride and encourage you to keep working towards your goals.

Surround yourself with positive people: Being around others who support and encourage you can have a huge impact on your motivation. Seek out friends and mentors who are positive, inspiring, and knowledgeable in your area of interest.

Keep learning: Learning new skills and acquiring new knowledge can help you stay motivated and engaged. Whether it's through taking courses, reading books, or simply trying new things, make sure to continuously challenge yourself and expand your knowledge and skills.

Take care of yourself: Taking care of your physical and mental health is key to staying motivated. Make sure to get enough sleep, eat well, exercise regularly, and practice self-care activities like meditation or yoga.

Stay organised: Having a clear plan for how you will achieve your goals, and breaking it down into smaller, manageable tasks can help you stay motivated and on track. Make a to-do list, use a planner or calendar, and prioritise tasks to help you stay organised and focused.

Focus on the process, not just the outcome: It's easy to get discouraged when you're focused solely on the end goal. Instead, try to enjoy the journey and appreciate the hard work and progress you're making along the way.

Stay flexible: Life is unpredictable and things don't always go as planned. It's important to be flexible and adaptable, and to be able to pivot your plans when necessary. This will help you stay motivated and avoid becoming discouraged by setbacks.

Stay positive: Keeping a positive outlook and focusing on the good in any situation can help you stay motivated and avoid getting bogged down by negativity. Try to focus on the opportunities and benefits that come with challenges, and look for ways to turn setbacks into opportunities for growth.

Reward yourself: Finally, don't forget to reward yourself for your hard work and progress. Whether it's taking a day off, treating yourself to a nice meal, or simply taking a moment to reflect on your accomplishments, make sure to celebrate your successes and give yourself credit for the progress you're making.

Staying motivated is not always easy, but with the right strategies and mindset, it is possible. By setting clear goals, celebrating your successes, surrounding yourself with positive people, and taking care of yourself, you can maintain your drive and stay focused on your objectives. Remember to enjoy the journey, stay flexible, and stay positive, and you'll be well on your way to achieving your goals and reaching your full potential.

Chapter 4

# Common Positive Habits

Positive habits are behaviours that bring us closer to our goals and help us live happier, healthier and more fulfilling lives. They are habits that are easy to adopt, provide instant benefits and can be turned into long-lasting and effective lifestyle changes. Here are some of the most common positive habits that people can adopt:

**Exercise:** Regular physical activity is one of the most important positive habits you can develop. Exercise helps improve your overall health and well-being, increase energy levels, and boost mood. It can also help you stay in shape and reduce the risk of chronic diseases such as heart disease, type 2 diabetes, and some types of cancer.

**Eating a healthy diet:** Eating a balanced and nutritious diet is another essential positive habit. Eating a diet rich in fruits, vegetables, whole grains, and lean protein can help maintain a healthy weight, lower the risk of chronic diseases, and increase energy levels.

**Drinking enough water:** Drinking enough water is crucial for overall health and well-being. It helps keep the body hydrated, improves skin health, boosts energy levels, and can help regulate body temperature. Aim to drink at least eight glasses of water per day to keep your body hydrated.

**Getting enough sleep:** Sleep is essential for good health and well-being. Lack of sleep can affect mood, energy levels, and productivity. Aim for seven to nine hours of sleep each night to ensure that you are well-rested and ready to tackle the day.

**Reading:** Reading is a great way to expand your knowledge and improve your mental agility. It also provides a way to escape reality and immerse yourself in new and exciting worlds. Make reading a daily habit by setting aside time each day to read, whether it be a book, newspaper, or magazine.

**Gratitude**: Practicing gratitude is one of the most effective ways to cultivate positive emotions and boost well-being. Make a habit of taking a few minutes each day to reflect on what you are grateful for. You can write down your thoughts in a journal or simply take a moment to reflect on your blessings.

**Mindfulness:** Mindfulness is the practice of being present in the moment and focusing on your thoughts and feelings without judgement. It can help reduce stress, increase focus, and improve overall well-being. Make a habit of taking a few minutes each day to practise mindfulness, whether through meditation, deep breathing, or simply being present in the moment.

**Journaling**: Writing in a journal is a great way to reflect on your thoughts and emotions and track your progress over time. Journaling can also help you identify patterns and behaviours that may be holding you back and provide a space to work through difficult emotions. Make a habit of writing in your journal for a few minutes each day.

**Connecting with others:** Building and maintaining relationships is important for overall health and well-being. Make a habit of reaching out to friends and family, and making an effort to connect with others in your community. Whether it's through phone calls, text messages, or in-person visits, connecting with others can bring joy and support to your life.

**Practising self-care:** Taking care of yourself is essential for good health and well-being. This can include activities such as getting enough sleep, eating a healthy diet, and engaging in physical activity. It can also include more self-indulgent activities such as taking a bath, getting a massage, or simply taking time for yourself to relax and recharge.

positive habits are essential for good health and well-being. They provide a way to make lasting changes in our lives and improve our overall happiness.

## Exercise and Physical Activity

Physical activity and exercise are crucial components of a healthy lifestyle. They play a significant role in maintaining good health, preventing various chronic diseases, improving mental health and overall quality of life. Regular exercise and physical activity are essential for all ages, from children to the elderly, as they provide numerous physical and mental health benefits.

Physical activity can be any type of movement that uses your muscles and increases your heart rate. It can be as simple as taking a walk, doing household chores, or playing with your children. Exercise, on the other hand, is a type of physical activity that is planned, structured, repetitive and has a specific goal, such as improving fitness or athletic performance. Exercise can be done in a variety of forms, including aerobics, strength training, yoga, and many others.

One of the most significant benefits of physical activity and exercise is their ability to improve cardiovascular health. Regular exercise can help lower blood pressure, improve cholesterol levels, and reduce the risk of heart disease and stroke. Exercise also helps to regulate blood sugar levels and reduces the risk of type 2 diabetes.

Strength training and resistance exercises are important for maintaining and building muscle mass, which can help improve overall strength, mobility and balance. This is particularly important for older adults, as muscle mass naturally decreases with age, making them more susceptible to falls and injuries. Strength training also helps to increase bone density, reducing the risk of osteoporosis.

Physical activity and exercise can also play a vital role in maintaining a healthy weight. Regular exercise helps to burn calories and increase metabolism, making it easier to maintain a healthy weight. Physical activity can also increase feelings of fullness and reduce hunger, helping to prevent overeating.

In addition to physical health benefits, regular exercise and physical activity can also have a positive impact on mental health. Exercise has been shown to reduce symptoms of depression, anxiety, and stress. Physical activity can increase the production of endorphins, which are natural painkillers and mood elevators. Exercise can also improve sleep quality, helping to reduce fatigue and improve overall well-being.

Physical activity can also be a fun and social activity. Engaging in physical activity with friends or family can be a great way to bond and stay connected with others. Group exercise classes and sports teams can provide a sense of community and social support, helping to improve overall mental health and well-being.

It is recommended that adults engage in at least 150 minutes of moderate-intensity aerobic exercise per week, or 75 minutes of vigorous-intensity aerobic exercise. Strength training exercises are recommended two or more times per week.

Children and adolescents should engage in at least 60 minutes of physical activity per day.

In conclusion, physical activity and exercise are essential components of a healthy lifestyle. They provide numerous physical and mental health benefits, including improved cardiovascular health, increased muscle strength, improved mental health, and better weight management. It is recommended that adults engage in at least 150 minutes of moderate-intensity aerobic exercise per week, and children and adolescents engage in at least 60 minutes of physical activity per day. So, make time for exercise and physical activity, and enjoy the numerous health benefits they provide.

## Healthy Eating and Hydration

Healthy eating and hydration are crucial components of overall health and wellness. A well-balanced diet that includes a variety of nutrient-dense foods and enough water intake can help support physical and mental health, prevent chronic diseases, and promote overall well-being.

A healthy diet should include a variety of food groups, including fruits, vegetables, whole grains, lean proteins, and healthy fats. Fruits and vegetables are excellent sources of vitamins, minerals, and fibre, and should make up a significant portion of your diet. Whole grains are a good source of carbohydrates and fibre and can help regulate blood sugar levels. Lean proteins, such as poultry, fish, and legumes, are important for muscle repair and growth, and can help keep you feeling full and satisfied. Healthy fats, such as those found in nuts, seeds, and avocados, provide energy and support brain health.

In addition to including these food groups in your diet, it's also important to limit processed foods and added sugars, as these can be high in calories and low in nutrients. Try to choose whole foods whenever possible, and limit your intake of sugary drinks and snacks.

Hydration is equally important for overall health. The human body is made up of 60% water, and it's essential for many of our physiological processes, including regulating body temperature, transporting nutrients, and flushing out waste. Most people need to drink at least eight glasses of water a day to maintain optimal hydration. However, the amount of water needed can vary based on factors such as age, activity level, and the climate you live in.

Drinking water can also help with weight management, as it can help you feel full and reduce the amount of calories consumed from other beverages and snacks. In addition, staying hydrated can improve physical performance and reduce fatigue, making it easier to maintain an active lifestyle.

If plain water isn't your thing, there are other options to help you stay hydrated. Herbal teas, sparkling water, and coconut water are all great alternatives to sugary drinks, and can help you meet your daily hydration needs.

It's also important to be mindful of the foods and drinks you consume that can lead to dehydration, such as caffeine and alcohol. Caffeine is a diuretic, meaning it can increase the need to urinate, which can lead to dehydration. Alcohol also dehydrates the body, so it's important to drink plenty of water when consuming alcohol.

healthy eating and hydration are key to overall health and well-being. By focusing on nutrient-dense foods, limiting processed foods and added sugars, and staying hydrated, you can support your physical and mental health and reduce your risk of chronic diseases. Make healthy eating and hydration a priority, and your body will thank you.

## Good Sleep Hygiene

Good sleep hygiene refers to habits and practices that promote restful and restorative sleep. A lack of good sleep hygiene can lead to sleep disturbances, sleep deprivation, and a range of health problems. On the other hand, good sleep hygiene practices can improve sleep quality and contribute to overall health and well-being. In this article, we will examine some key principles of good sleep hygiene and how to implement them in your daily life.

Establish a consistent sleep schedule: Going to bed and waking up at the same time every day helps regulate your circadian rhythm, the natural biological process that regulates sleep and wakefulness. Try to stick to your sleep schedule as closely as possible, even on weekends.

Create a sleep-conducive environment: Your sleeping environment should be dark, quiet, and cool, with a comfortable mattress and pillows. Use earplugs or a white noise machine to block out any distracting sounds, and consider investing in blackout curtains or a sleep mask to block out light.

Limit exposure to screens before bedtime: The blue light emitted by screens on devices like phones, tablets, and televisions can suppress the production of the sleep hormone melatonin, making it harder to fall asleep. Try to avoid using screens for at least an hour before bedtime, or invest in blue light blocking glasses or a screen filter.

Avoid caffeine, nicotine, and alcohol: Caffeine, nicotine, and alcohol are stimulants that can interfere with sleep. Try to avoid consuming these substances in the hours leading up to bedtime.

**Exercise regularly:** Regular physical activity can promote better sleep, but it's important to avoid strenuous exercise close to bedtime, as it can make it harder to fall asleep. Aim to exercise at least 30 minutes a day, but earlier in the day if possible.

**Avoid napping during the day:** Napping during the day can interfere with nighttime sleep, especially if it's done close to bedtime. If you feel the need to nap, try to limit it to 20-30 minutes earlier in the day.

**Relax before bedtime**: Winding down before bedtime can help prepare your body for sleep. Try reading a book, listening to calming music, taking a warm bath, or practising relaxation techniques like deep breathing or progressive muscle relaxation.

**Limit time spent in bed awake:** If you find yourself lying in bed awake for more than 20-30 minutes, get out of bed and engage in a quiet activity until you feel sleepy. This helps to associate your bed with sleep, making it easier to fall asleep.

 good sleep hygiene is essential for improving sleep quality and promoting overall health and well-being. By establishing a consistent sleep schedule, creating a sleep-conducive environment, limiting exposure to screens, avoiding stimulants, exercising regularly, avoiding napping, relaxing before bedtime, and limiting time spent in bed awake, you can improve your sleep hygiene and get the restful and restorative sleep you need.

Remember that everyone's sleep needs are different, so what works for one person may not work for another. If you're having trouble sleeping despite following good sleep hygiene practices, it's important to speak with your healthcare provider to rule out any underlying medical conditions that may be affecting your sleep.

## Meditation and Mindfulness

Meditation and mindfulness are practices that have been around for thousands of years, originating in ancient spiritual and religious traditions. In recent years, these practices have gained popularity as a way to reduce stress and improve mental well-being. Both meditation and mindfulness aim to help individuals focus their attention on the present moment, quiet their minds, and develop a more positive and relaxed state of being.

Meditation involves intentionally focusing one's attention, often on a specific object, sound, or physical sensation, while disregarding distractions and letting thoughts come and go without judgement. The aim is to cultivate a state of deep concentration and awareness. Meditation can be practised in a variety of forms, including mindfulness meditation, loving-kindness meditation, body scan meditation, and guided visualisation, among others. Practising meditation on a regular basis can help individuals develop greater focus, concentration, and self-awareness.

Mindfulness, on the other hand, is a state of being present in the moment, fully engaged in one's thoughts, feelings, and physical sensations without judgement. It involves paying attention to the present moment, without being caught up in thoughts about the past or future. Mindfulness can be cultivated through meditation, but it can also be practised in everyday activities, such as eating, walking, or washing dishes.

Research has shown that both meditation and mindfulness have a number of benefits for mental health and well-being. For example, they have been shown to reduce stress, anxiety, and depression, improve sleep quality, boost the immune system, and increase overall happiness and life satisfaction. Additionally, mindfulness has been shown to help individuals manage chronic pain, lower blood pressure, and improve cognitive functioning, such as memory and attention.

In order to get the most out of meditation and mindfulness, it is important to make them a regular part of one's routine. Starting with just a few minutes a day is a good way to build the habit, and gradually increasing the length and frequency of the practice can lead to greater benefits. There is no one right way to practise meditation and mindfulness, so it is important to experiment and find what works best for each individual.

While both meditation and mindfulness can be powerful tools for improving mental health and well-being, it is important to remember that they are not a cure-all and may not be suitable for everyone. Some individuals may find that they have difficulty quieting their minds or staying focused, while others may struggle with the judgement-free aspect of the practices. In these cases, it may be helpful to seek the guidance of a trained therapist or teacher.

In conclusion, meditation and mindfulness are ancient practices that have been gaining popularity in recent years as a way to improve mental health and well-being. Both practices involve focusing one's attention on the present moment, quieting the mind, and developing a more positive and relaxed state of being. Regular practice has been shown to have a number of benefits, including reducing stress, boosting the immune system, and improving cognitive functioning. While these practices can be powerful tools, it is important to remember that they are not a cure-all and may not be suitable for everyone.

## Gratitude and Positive Thinking

Gratitude and positive thinking are two of the most powerful tools for improving our mental and emotional wellbeing. They are interconnected, and each can support and amplify the other. Gratitude helps us to focus on the good things in our lives, and positive thinking helps us to see the world in a more optimistic light. Together, they can help us to build resilience, increase our happiness and satisfaction, and lead a more fulfilling life.

Gratitude is a feeling of thankfulness or appreciation for what we have, or for things that have happened to us. Research has shown that expressing gratitude regularly can have a significant impact on our wellbeing. It can reduce stress, increase happiness, and improve our relationships with others. When we focus on what we are grateful for, we are less likely to dwell on what is lacking in our lives, and this can help us to see the world in a more positive light.

Gratitude can be practised in many ways. One of the simplest is to keep a gratitude journal, in which you write down a few things each day that you are thankful for. This could be as simple as being grateful for a sunny day, or for having a roof over your head. Alternatively, you might express gratitude by saying thank you to people who have helped you, or by sending a card or note to someone who has made a positive impact on your life.

Positive thinking, on the other hand, involves looking for the positive in every situation, and focusing on the good rather than the bad. Positive thinking can help us to develop a more optimistic outlook, and to cope better with challenges and setbacks. When we approach life with a positive attitude, we are less likely to be discouraged by obstacles, and more likely to be motivated to find solutions and overcome difficulties.

Positive thinking is a habit that can be developed with practice. Start by focusing on the positive aspects of your life, and on the good things that happen to you. Try to avoid negative thoughts and replace them with positive ones. For example, instead of thinking "I'll never get that job", try thinking "I'll find a job that's a better fit for me". Focus on your strengths, and be kind to yourself.

When you make a mistake, try to view it as an opportunity for growth and learning, rather than as a failure.

Gratitude and positive thinking are powerful in their own right, but they are even more effective when used together. Gratitude can help us to focus on the good in our lives, and positive thinking can help us to see the good in every situation. When we combine the two, we can develop a more optimistic outlook, and build resilience in the face of adversity.

In conclusion, gratitude and positive thinking are two essential tools for improving our wellbeing. They can help us to reduce stress, increase happiness, and lead a more fulfilling life. By incorporating these practices into our daily lives, we can cultivate a more positive and grateful attitude, and create a more supportive and uplifting environment for ourselves and those around us.

# Chapter 5

# Overcoming Negative Habits

Negative habits can have a significant impact on our lives, causing stress, decreased productivity, and even health problems. However, breaking these habits is not always easy and requires discipline, patience, and a plan. Here are some steps to help you overcome negative habits and make positive changes in your life:

- **Identify the root cause:** Understanding the root cause of a negative habit is essential in overcoming it. It could be stress, boredom, anxiety, or a lack of self-esteem, among others. Once you understand the underlying issue, you can work on finding alternative ways to cope.

- **Set achievable goals**: Breaking a negative habit requires setting achievable goals. Start small and gradually increase the difficulty of your goals as you progress. Setting achievable goals will help you stay motivated and focused on your progress.

- **Find a replacement activity:** Find an activity that you can do instead of engaging in the negative habit. This could be anything from exercise to reading a book. The key is to find something that is enjoyable and that you can look forward to doing instead of the negative habit.

- Having a supportive network of friends and family members who encourage and support you in your efforts to overcome a negative habit can be extremely helpful. Surrounding yourself with positive people will give you the strength and motivation you need to succeed.

- **Track your progress:** Keeping track of your progress is essential in overcoming negative habits. Use a journal or an app to record your progress, and celebrate each small victory along the way. This will help you stay focused and motivated.

- **Be patient and persistent:** Overcoming negative habits takes time and effort, and there will likely be setbacks along the way. Be patient and persistent, and don't give up even when it feels like you're not making progress. Remember that change is a gradual process, and that it takes time to develop new, positive habits.

- **Seek support**: If you find that you're struggling to overcome a negative habit on your own, consider seeking support from a professional. A therapist or counsellor can provide you with tools and strategies to help you overcome your negative habit, as well as support and encouragement along the way.

The power of breaking negative habits is not always easy, but it is possible with the right mindset and approach. By identifying the root cause, setting achievable goals, finding a replacement activity, surrounding yourself with positive people, tracking your progress, being patient and persistent, and seeking support, you can overcome negative habits and make positive changes in your life. Remember, the key is to take small steps and be consistent in your efforts. Good luck!

## Understanding Negative Habits

Negative habits are behaviours that are harmful to our well-being, either physically or mentally, and can negatively impact our daily lives. These habits can range from biting our nails, procrastination, overspending, smoking, and many others.

To understand negative habits, it's important to consider the underlying causes and motivations behind them. Often, negative habits serve as coping mechanisms for stress, anxiety, or other difficult emotions. For example, overeating may be a way to temporarily distract from feelings of loneliness or boredom.

Additionally, negative habits can become ingrained through repetition and can be difficult to break without a deeper understanding of why they exist in the first place. For instance, someone who has a habit of smoking may not initially realise the impact it has on their health, and may continue the behaviour without considering the long-term consequences.

To effectively change negative habits, it's important to first identify them and understand why they are problematic. This can be done through self-reflection or seeking the help of a therapist or counsellor. It's also crucial to establish new habits that can replace the negative ones, such as finding healthy ways to cope with stress or finding alternative ways to spend time and money.

For example, someone who has a habit of procrastination can begin to break it by setting small, achievable goals and taking action towards them, as well as learning time management techniques and breaking tasks into smaller steps. Someone who struggles with overspending can learn about budgeting and saving, and find alternative ways to spend their time that don't involve spending money.

Moreover, it's important to have self-compassion and to be kind to yourself when working on breaking negative habits. Change is not easy and setbacks may occur, but it's important to remember that progress is not linear, and to continue working towards your goals.

It's also helpful to have a support system in place, such as a friend or family member who can provide encouragement and accountability. Joining a support group or participating in therapy can also be useful in breaking negative habits and developing healthy habits.

understanding negative habits is the first step in breaking them and living a happier, healthier life. It's important to identify the underlying causes and motivations, establish new habits to replace the negative ones, be kind to yourself, and have a support system in place. With time and effort, it's possible to overcome negative habits and lead a fulfilling life.

## Strategies for Overcoming Negative Habits

Negative habits can be challenging to overcome, but with the right strategies, it is possible to change them for good. Here are some effective methods for overcoming negative habits:

**Identify the root cause:** Understanding the root cause of your negative habit is crucial to overcoming it. Ask yourself why you engage in this behaviour, and consider any underlying emotional or psychological issues that may be contributing to it.

**Set achievable goals:** Setting realistic and achievable goals for yourself can help you stay motivated as you work to overcome your negative habit. Write down your goals and make a plan for how you will reach them.

**Replace the habit with a positive one:** Instead of simply trying to stop a negative habit, try to replace it with a positive one. For example, if you have a habit of snacking on junk food when you're stressed, try to replace that with a healthy habit like going for a walk or doing yoga.

**Build a support system:** Surround yourself with supportive friends and family members who will encourage and help you overcome your negative habit. You can also join support groups or work with a therapist who can help you navigate the process.

**Practice mindfulness:** Mindfulness can help you become more aware of your thoughts, feelings, and actions, which can be particularly helpful in overcoming negative habits. Try to live in the moment and be mindful of your thoughts, feelings, and behaviours.

**Use positive self-talk:** The way you talk to yourself can have a big impact on your success in overcoming negative habits. Practice speaking to yourself in a positive and encouraging way, and focus on your strengths and achievements.

**Reward yourself:** Celebrate your successes along the way. Set up a reward system for yourself as you work to overcome your negative habit, and reward yourself for meeting your goals.

**Be patient:** Overcoming a negative habit takes time, so it's important to be patient with yourself. Don't be too hard on yourself if you slip up, but instead, use it as an opportunity to learn and grow.

**Keep track of your progress:** Keeping track of your progress can help you stay motivated and see how far you've come. Write down your progress and celebrate your successes along the way.

**Stay committed:** Overcoming a negative habit requires a lot of effort and dedication. Stay committed to your goals, and don't give up even when it gets difficult.

overcoming negative habits can be a challenging process, but it is possible with the right strategies. By identifying the root cause, setting achievable goals, replacing the habit with a positive one, building a support system, practising mindfulness, using positive self-talk, rewarding yourself, being patient, keeping track of your progress, and staying committed, you can overcome any negative habit and improve your life.

## Staying Focused and Committed

Staying focused and committed are important traits to have in order to be successful in anything you set your mind to. Whether it's at work, school, or in your personal life, staying focused and committed can help you achieve your goals, overcome obstacles, and lead a more productive and fulfilling life. However, it can be challenging to maintain focus and commitment, especially in a world that is constantly vying for our attention. Here are some tips to help you stay focused and committed:

Set clear and attainable goals: One of the best ways to stay focused and committed is to set clear and attainable goals. Write down what you want to achieve and break it down into smaller, manageable tasks. This will give you a roadmap to follow and help you stay on track.

**Stay organised**: It's difficult to stay focused and committed if you're feeling overwhelmed or disorganised. Take the time to organize your workspace and your life in general. This will help you stay on track and reduce distractions.

**Eliminate distractions:** Distractions are the enemy of focus and commitment. Identify the sources of distraction in your life and find ways to eliminate or minimise them. This might include turning off notifications on your phone, closing your email during certain times of the day, or working in a quiet environment.

**Prioritise your tasks:** In order to stay focused and committed, it's important to prioritize your tasks. Determine which tasks are most important and focus on them first. This will help you make the most of your time and ensure that you're making progress towards your goals.

**Stay motivated:** Staying motivated is key to staying focused and committed. Find ways to motivate yourself, such as setting small rewards for completing tasks, connecting with a supportive community, or reminding yourself why you're working towards your goals in the first place.

**Take breaks:** It's important to take breaks in order to stay focused and committed. Taking a short break can help you recharge and refocus, making it easier to stay on track.

**Stay disciplined:** Staying disciplined is critical to staying focused and committed. Make a plan and stick to it. Keep yourself accountable and hold yourself to a high standard.

**Stay positive:** A positive outlook is key to staying focused and committed. Surround yourself with positive people, avoid negative self-talk, and focus on the things you can control.

**Be adaptable:** While it's important to have a plan, it's equally important to be adaptable. Life is unpredictable, and sometimes things don't go as planned. Be open to change and be willing to pivot when necessary.

**Celebrate your successes:** Celebrating your successes is an important part of staying focused and committed. Recognize your achievements, no matter how small, and take the time to celebrate your progress.

In conclusion, staying focused and committed requires discipline, motivation, and a positive outlook. By setting clear and attainable goals, staying organised, eliminating distractions, prioritising your tasks, taking breaks, and being adaptable, you can stay focused and committed to achieving your goals. Celebrating your successes along the way is an important part of the process, as it helps you stay motivated and maintain your focus.

# Chapter 6

## Maintaining Positive Habits

Maintaining positive habits is a key aspect of leading a fulfilling and productive life. Habits are patterns of behaviour that are performed regularly and automatically, and they can either be positive or negative. Positive habits, such as exercising regularly, eating a healthy diet, and staying organised, can lead to improved physical and mental well-being, while negative habits, such as procrastination, overeating, and engaging in unhealthy activities, can have the opposite effect.

To maintain positive habits, it is important to understand why you want to form these habits in the first place. Having a clear motivation and purpose can help provide you with the necessary motivation to stick to your habits, even when the going gets tough. For example, if you want to exercise regularly to improve your physical health, it can be helpful to remind yourself of your goal whenever you feel discouraged or unmotivated.

Another important factor in maintaining positive habits is to make them a part of your routine. Habits are most easily formed and maintained when they are performed regularly and at the same time each day. For example, if you want to start exercising every morning, try to get up at the same time each day and start your workout at the same time each morning. Over time, this routine will become automatic, and you will find it easier to maintain your habit.

In addition to making your habits a part of your routine, it is also important to make them achievable and realistic. Starting with small, manageable goals and gradually increasing their difficulty as you become more comfortable with the habit can help you avoid becoming discouraged or overwhelmed. For example, if you want to start exercising regularly, you could start with a 10-minute walk every day and gradually increase the length and intensity of your workout over time.

Another important factor in maintaining positive habits is to track your progress. Keeping a record of your habit-forming progress can help you stay motivated and on track. For example, if you want to start eating a healthier diet, you could keep a food journal to track what you eat each day. This journal can help you identify areas where you need to make changes, and it can also help you see how far you have come over time.

Finally, it is important to be patient and persistent when forming and maintaining positive habits. Habits take time to form, and it is normal to encounter setbacks and challenges along the way. The key is to not give up and to keep pushing forward, even when it feels difficult. Celebrating your successes, no matter how small, can help you stay motivated and keep moving forward.

maintaining positive habits requires a combination of self-awareness, motivation, routine, achievable goals, tracking progress, and persistence. By focusing on these key elements, you can form habits that will improve your physical and mental well-being and help you lead a fulfilling and productive life. So if you are looking to improve your life, start by forming positive habits and stick with them over time.

# Monitoring Progress

Monitoring progress is an essential aspect of any project, goal or task, as it helps in tracking the performance, status, and results of the work being done. It helps individuals and organisations to make informed decisions, evaluate the success of their initiatives and adjust their approach if needed. Monitoring progress can take place at different levels, from individual projects to entire organisations.

When monitoring progress, it is important to establish specific, measurable, and time-bound goals. These goals serve as a reference point, making it easier to evaluate progress and determine if changes are needed. In order to monitor progress effectively, it is important to have a clear understanding of the starting point, the desired end state and the steps required to reach the desired outcome. This includes having a clear understanding of what data is needed and how to collect it.

Data collection is a critical component of progress monitoring. This can include anything from tracking hours worked to analysing sales data, and it is important to choose the right metrics to measure progress. The metrics should be meaningful, relevant, and measurable, and should be reviewed on a regular basis. Progress monitoring can be done through various methods, including manual tracking, spreadsheets, and specialised software, depending on the needs and resources of the organisation.

Regular feedback is another important component of monitoring progress. Feedback provides insight into the performance of the project, the team and the individuals involved, and can help identify areas for improvement. Feedback can be provided in a variety of formats, including performance evaluations, project updates, and one-on-one meetings. It is important to encourage open and honest feedback, as this can lead to improvements and better results.

Another important aspect of progress monitoring is the ability to make informed decisions. This requires analysing data, identifying trends and patterns, and using this information to adjust the approach and approach. For example, if sales data indicates a slowdown, it may be necessary to make changes to the marketing strategy or the product offering. Monitoring progress enables organisations to make informed decisions that can have a positive impact on the outcome of the project.

When monitoring progress, it is important to be proactive and take action if progress is not on track. This can involve taking steps to correct any problems, such as addressing issues with team members or adjusting the approach to the project. It is also important to be flexible and adaptable, as progress monitoring may reveal that changes are needed to meet the desired outcomes.

Monitoring progress is an essential aspect of achieving success in any project, goal or task. It provides a means of tracking performance, identifying areas for improvement, and making informed decisions. Regular data collection, feedback, and analysis are critical components of effective progress monitoring, and organisations should be proactive and flexible in their approach to ensure they are on track to meet their goals. Effective progress monitoring requires a clear understanding of the goals, a well-defined plan, and the ability to collect and analyse relevant data, as well as the flexibility to make changes as needed.

# Celebrating Successes

Celebrating success is an important part of the human experience. It's a time to reflect on the hard work and determination that went into achieving a goal, and to acknowledge the achievements of others. Whether it's a personal milestone, such as losing weight or quitting smoking, or a professional achievement, such as landing a new job or completing a project, the act of celebrating success can provide a sense of satisfaction and motivation to continue pushing forward.

There are many different ways to celebrate success, and the method you choose will depend on your personal preferences, the type of achievement, and the people involved. Some popular options include:

**Throwing a party or celebration event:** This is a classic way to mark a milestone or achievement.

Whether it's a small gathering of friends or a large-scale celebration, a party can be a fun and festive way to mark a special occasion.

**Treating yourself**: If you've achieved a personal goal, such as losing weight or running a marathon, treating yourself to something special can be a great way to reward yourself for your hard work. This could be a spa day, a shopping spree, or a fancy dinner.

**Recognizing others**: Celebrating success is also about acknowledging the achievements of others. If you're part of a team that has accomplished something great, recognizing the contributions of each team member can help build morale and foster a sense of teamwork.

**Giving back**: Celebrating success can also be an opportunity to give back to others. If you've achieved a significant financial goal, for example, consider donating a portion of your winnings to a charity or non-profit organisation.

**Taking time for yourself:** Taking a break and enjoying some well-deserved "me time" is another way to celebrate success. This could involve taking a vacation, reading a book, or simply relaxing and unwinding.

Celebrating success is important for a number of reasons. For one, it helps you acknowledge the hard work and determination that went into achieving a goal. This can be especially valuable if you've been working towards a goal for a long period of time. Celebrating success can also provide a sense of motivation and inspiration, as you reflect on what you've accomplished and consider what you'd like to achieve in the future.

In addition, celebrating success can also help build morale and foster a sense of teamwork and community. Whether you're part of a team at work or a group of friends who have all accomplished something great, taking the time to recognize each other's achievements can help build strong, supportive relationships.

Finally, celebrating success can also help build confidence and self-esteem. By acknowledging your own achievements and the achievements of others, you can develop a stronger sense of self-worth and become more resilient in the face of challenges and setbacks.

In conclusion, celebrating success is an important part of the human experience. Whether you're marking a personal milestone or a professional achievement, taking the time to acknowledge and reward yourself for your hard work can provide a sense of satisfaction, motivation, and inspiration. So go ahead, celebrate your successes - you deserve it!

# Staying On Track

Staying on track is an essential aspect of life. Whether it be personal or professional, everyone has goals that they want to achieve, and staying on track is crucial for success. In this article, we will be discussing the various ways in which one can stay on track and achieve their goals.

**Setting Clear Goals:** The first and most important step in staying on track is setting clear and concise goals. It's important to have a clear vision of what you want to achieve, and the steps that you need to take to get there. When setting your goals, it's important to make sure they are SMART: Specific, Measurable, Achievable, Relevant, and Time-bound.

**Creating a Plan:** Once you have set your goals, the next step is to create a plan to achieve them. Your plan should include a timeline, actionable steps, and milestones to keep you on track. This plan should be reviewed regularly to ensure that you are making progress and to make any necessary adjustments.

**Breaking Down Tasks**: Another important step in staying on track is breaking down large tasks into smaller, more manageable parts. This will make it easier for you to focus on each step and to see progress along the way. Breaking down tasks also helps to reduce the feeling of overwhelm and can increase motivation.

**Time Management**: Time management is key to staying on track. Making the most of your time will allow you to get more done in less time, and will also reduce stress. A useful technique is to prioritize tasks and to work on the most important ones first. This will ensure that you are making progress on your goals and will help you to stay focused.

**Staying Organized:** Keeping your environment organised can help you to stay on track. A cluttered workspace can be distracting and make it difficult to focus. It's important to keep your workspace clean and tidy, and to have a system for organising your work and tasks. This will help you to stay focused and to make progress on your goals.

**Surrounding Yourself with Positive People**: Surrounding yourself with positive people can have a huge impact on your ability to stay on track. Positive people can provide support and encouragement, and can help you to stay motivated. They can also provide new perspectives and ideas that can help you to achieve your goals.

**Staying Motivated**: Staying motivated is a crucial part of staying on track. There will be times when you feel discouraged or overwhelmed, but it's important to push through these times and to stay focused on your goals. One way to stay motivated is to remind yourself of why you started and to celebrate your successes along the way.

**Keeping a Journal**: Keeping a journal can be a helpful tool in staying on track. Writing down your goals, your progress, and any obstacles that you encounter can help you to see the bigger picture and to stay focused. Reviewing your journal regularly can also help you to stay motivated and to make any necessary adjustments to your plan.

staying on track is an important aspect of achieving success. By setting clear goals, creating a plan, breaking down tasks, managing your time, staying organised, surrounding yourself with positive people, staying motivated, and keeping a journal, you can increase your chances of staying on track and achieving your goals. Remember to be patient and persistent, and to celebrate your successes along the way.

# Conclusion

Positive habits play a crucial role in shaping an individual's life and helping them reach their full potential. It has been scientifically proven that consistent engagement in positive habits leads to improved physical, mental, and emotional health, greater life satisfaction, and a stronger sense of purpose.

Starting with small, achievable actions can help to establish positive habits and make them a permanent part of one's daily routine. This could be as simple as waking up early, exercising regularly, meditating, practising gratitude, and eating a nutritious diet. These habits not only benefit one's physical health but also promote a positive mindset and improve one's overall sense of well-being.

Maintaining a positive outlook, regardless of the challenges life may bring, is also a vital aspect of positive habits. This means actively seeking out the good in situations and focusing on the positives rather than dwelling on the negatives. Engaging in activities that bring joy and fulfilment, such as hobbies, spending time with loved ones, or volunteering, can also help to cultivate a positive mindset.

Positive habits also play a crucial role in developing strong relationships and promoting effective communication. Regularly expressing appreciation, actively listening, and being respectful towards others can help to build and maintain healthy relationships. Positive habits such as empathy and kindness also have a ripple effect and can have a significant impact on the people around us, creating a positive and supportive community.

In conclusion, positive habits have far-reaching benefits for individuals and society as a whole. By consistently engaging in these habits, we can improve our physical, mental, and emotional health, build strong relationships, and lead fulfilling lives. Cultivating positive habits is an ongoing process and requires dedication, but the rewards are immeasurable. So, let us strive to make positive habits a permanent part of our daily routines, and watch as our lives transform for the better.

# The Power of Positive Habits for a Better Life

Positive habits are the key to a better life. They are simple, small, and repeated actions that can bring about big changes in our lives. When we establish positive habits, we create a powerful foundation for success, happiness, and well-being. Here, we'll explore the power of positive habits and how they can help us lead a better life.

One of the most significant benefits of positive habits is that they help us develop self-discipline. Self-discipline is the ability to control our thoughts, emotions, and behaviours. When we engage in positive habits, we train our minds to resist temptation and focus on what's important. This helps us to overcome procrastination and distractions, so we can achieve our goals.

Another benefit of positive habits is that they help us cultivate a growth mindset. A growth mindset is the belief that our abilities and intelligence can be developed through effort and dedication. When we engage in positive habits, we demonstrate to ourselves that we can change, grow, and improve. This can lead to greater resilience and persistence in the face of challenges and obstacles.

Positive habits can also help us improve our physical and mental health. Regular exercise, healthy eating, and adequate sleep are all positive habits that can improve our overall well-being. By taking care of our bodies, we also take care of our minds, which can help us be more productive and focused.

In addition to improving our physical and mental health, positive habits can also improve our relationships. Positive habits such as active listening, empathy, and gratitude can help us connect with others on a deeper level. By building strong relationships, we can create a support network of people who are there for us when we need them.

Finally, positive habits can help us cultivate happiness and contentment. When we engage in activities that bring us joy, we can improve our mood and increase our overall life satisfaction. This can lead to a more positive outlook on life, which can help us to overcome difficulties and find meaning in our lives.

In conclusion, positive habits are a powerful tool for improving our lives. They help us develop self-discipline, cultivate a growth mindset, improve our physical and mental health, improve our relationships, and increase our happiness and contentment. By developing positive habits, we can create a foundation for success and well-being that will serve us for years to come. So, start small, be consistent, and enjoy the many benefits that positive habits can bring to your life.

## Final Thoughts and Recommendations

Positive habits can be defined as those actions and behaviours that are aligned with our goals and values, and have a positive impact on our well-being and those around us. They can range from healthy eating habits, regular exercise, practising mindfulness and gratitude, to time management and effective communication skills. Incorporating positive habits into our daily routine can help us lead a fulfilling life and improve our physical, mental, and emotional health.

However, developing positive habits is not an easy feat and requires a lot of discipline, determination, and persistence. Here are some final thoughts and recommendations for establishing positive habits:

**Start Small:** One of the biggest mistakes people make when trying to develop a positive habit is to take on too much too soon. It's better to start small and gradually build up rather than trying to change everything at once. For example, if you want to establish a habit of exercising every day, start with a 10-minute walk, and gradually increase the duration and intensity.

**Be Consistent**: Consistency is key to forming any habit. It's essential to stick to your routine every day, even on days when you don't feel like it. Over time, the actions and behaviours that you repeat become automatic, and you will do them without thinking.

**Track Your Progress:** Keeping track of your progress can be an excellent motivator. Write down your goals and what you have accomplished each day. Celebrate your successes, and use your failures as opportunities to learn and grow.

**Find an Accountability Partner:** Having someone to hold you accountable can help you stay motivated and committed to your positive habits. Find someone who shares similar goals, and who will support and encourage you along the way.

**Be Mindful of Your Thoughts:** Our thoughts and beliefs play a crucial role in shaping our habits. It's essential to be mindful of our thoughts and to challenge negative or limiting beliefs that may hold us back. Replace them with positive, empowering thoughts that support your goals and help you achieve your desired outcomes.

**Reward Yourself:** It's important to acknowledge and celebrate your progress and milestones along the way. Reward yourself for your efforts and achievements, whether it's a relaxing spa day, a night out with friends, or a new pair of shoes.

**Stay Positive:** Building positive habits takes time, effort, and patience. It's essential to stay positive and focus on the progress you have made, rather than dwelling on the challenges and setbacks.

developing positive habits is a journey, not a destination. It requires time, effort, and commitment, but the rewards are well worth it. Remember, habits are formed through repetition, and it takes time for new behaviours to become automatic. Be patient, stay focused, and stay committed to your goals, and you will see the results you desire.

Some of the key recommendations for establishing positive habits include starting small, being consistent, tracking your progress, finding an accountability partner, being mindful of your thoughts, rewarding yourself, and staying positive. Incorporating these habits into your daily routine can help you lead a healthier, happier, and more fulfilling life. GOOD LUCK!!!

www.ingramcontent.com/pod-product-compliance
Lightning Source LLC
Chambersburg PA
CBHW071139220526
45467CB00015B/1526